Quartet

THE BOOKSMYTH

Shelburne Falls, MA

2012

Quartet
four seasons in verse

Elisabeth Leete

The Booksmyth, Shelburne Falls, Massachusetts
www.gingercatpress.net   thebooksmyth@aol.com

ISBN 978-0-9815830-5-1

WITH GRATITUDE TO
My daughter Lucy Leete, who helped me with at least a thousand and one editing and computer details.

Maureen Moore, without whom this book would not have been possible.

Robert Parati, the talented artist who made the exquisite pictures enhancing the text.

All the friends who listened to me and encouraged me in countless writing workshops or conversations.

Artwork by Robert Parati
Book and cover design by Maureen Moore

Sometimes I think in French
sometimes I think in English
but most of the time
I think in gibberish.

~Elisabeth Leete

CONTENTS

WINTER *Largo-Adagio-Grave*
Silence 11
The Poem 12
The Box 13
Out 14
Pablo Neruda 15
Questions 16
Up or Down 17
Meditation 18
A Simple Death 19

SPRING *Allegro-Menuet*
Early Spring 23
My Garden 24
Have You Ever Seen 25
The Goldfinch 26
If 27
Courage 28
A Walk 29
To Lucy 30
Spring Cleaning 31
The Leopard and the White Star 32
Everything Is for the Best 33
In the Middle of March 34
Slow 35

SUMMER *Moderato-Suave*

By the Pond 39

The Inn 40

Happiness 41

Travails of a House Owner 42

Words 43

Do Not Worry 44

I Am 45

These Hands 46

AUTUMN *Andante*

Dear Little Pen 49

Mourning 50

November is Here, My Love 51

The House Was a Landscape 52

The Shoe 53

Grating Carrots 54

When the Gate Opened 55

Why Do I Write 56

A Night in Late Autumn 58

WINTER

Largo-Adagio-Grave

SILENCE

I have begun to re-learn
the beauty of silence.
Silence between lines,
silence between notes,
silence of night and morning.

Silence of the fire dying down,
of birds in wintertime.
Silence between words,
between thoughts.
Silence of the cold white moon
and of the hot summer sun.

Silence of the dog by my bed
and of a cat who never purrs.

Silence of the road at night,
silence of snow.

Silence of death,
blessed silence.

Silence of God.

THE POEM

May it open a thousand doors,
be the first line of a symphony,
dust the crumbs off the table
and make the coffee brew
while the mind is at rest.

Make it become a Hers or a His and salute
the solemn winter trees
along the snowy road.

Make it dry children's tears and silence
planes and trucks.

Ask him or her to drop
crystals and pearls
from high and divine places.

THE BOX

A little cardboard box,
dark blue,
twelve square inches,
this is what is left of you.

Where is your mind?
Where is your soul?
Where is your love?

OUT

The room is just the same,
    the same as before:

the simple, built-in furniture,
    the pictures of you,
    the pictures of me.

One day I took a mop and
    washed the walls
    and the ceiling.

I took the pictures of you
    and the pictures of me
    and I cleaned them.

I took the bright blue
    bedspread out and
    shook the dust out.

Pablo Neruda

There was life,
the sounds of multitudes.
There was passion for justice,
there was love and there was hatred.
There was the unbearable rhythm,
the killing staccato of war.

There were the waves of the ocean,
the tides of hope and glory,
the crescendos in the passion for hope,
the diminuendos, the crashes into despair,
the thunder of furious guns.

There were the tangos,
the waltzes of daily life,
the unfulfilled dreams, the unfinished work.
Moments of trivial desire, exalted times of joy,
flutes in the forests, wolves in the bushes.

QUESTIONS

A *T* can live without its bar,
an *I* without its dot,
a dog without its tail,
a man without his legs.

A question can end with no answer,
a meal without dessert.

A chicken can run without a head.

People can draw without toes,
     eat with tubes,
     sing with pens,
     smile with hands,
     drive with feet,
     dance on their heads.

Can a heart be split in two
Like an apple or pear?

Up or Down?

Something within me tells me I want to die.
Something within me tells me I want to live.
Something within me tells me
just relax.
Lie down and wait to die.

Something within me tells me "Hi"!
Wake up! Exercise! Make music!
You are all screwed up.
Make up your mind!

Something within me tells me
I like being screwed up,
being pulled up by life, down by death.
Or should it be pulled down by life,
pulled up by death?

MEDITATION

I told my body to find peace
but my body kept forgetting.

I tried to make the trivial moment vital
but the next moment kept encroaching.

I breathed deeply while counting
but mundane thoughts kept interfering.

I asked my pain to go away
but my pain said I shall not leave.

I savored the divine offering from my spring
till the gods said they preferred wine.

I begged my heart to fly me to heaven
but its wings kept fluttering
like the wings of a dying butterfly.

I tried to be one with the delphinium
but the lupine invited my eye.

A Simple Death

"I began to look at my life," my husband said to me. "What kind of person I had been to myself, to other people. I was inclined in these thoughts to examine myself pretty critically—things I had done that I wasn't proud of—how I had failed others, other people, people close to me."

In August 1990, my husband and I signed up for hospice care. Gurdon's prostate cancer had spread to his bones, causing excruciating pain and loss of weight. He could still walk a little with his cane and his mind was clear. On a sunny, warm afternoon and having nothing pressing to do—a rare moment in the life of a caregiver—I suggested we tape a conversation to give Gurdon a chance to share some of his thoughts about approaching death. He died three months later, on November 12, a day of cold, pale sunshine with Canadian geese in perfect triangular formation noisily crisscrossing the blue sky.

I recently found a yellowed transcript of the conversation, which was frequently interrupted to let Gurdon catch his breath. I was, again, impressed and touched by his humility, sincerity, quiet acceptance of death. Our daily routine was punctuated with visits from hospice nurses, home health aides and volunteers. No matter how he felt, Gurdon always asked his visitors how they were, and what about their families? Their jobs? And he always thanked them for each mundane task they helped him with. I asked him how he felt about saying thank you so many times every day. He said:

"I have always had the fault, I think, of feeling one has to reciprocate in some way. I feel a great need for reciprocity, or at least finding some way of demonstrating my appreciation for the great thoughtfulness of people I don't even know well." He continued:

"This period before death is very interesting and very rewarding. Sometimes it feels full of details, sometimes very contemplative, but most rewarding is the feeling of being surrounded by love and warmth; also the feeling that this is an ongoing process of life. It's good."

I asked him how he felt in the evening before going to sleep and in the morning when he woke up.

"Are there times when you hope this night may be the last?"

"Yes," he said. "This a comforting thought . . . and now, if you don't mind, let us pause for a moment."

SPRING

Allegro-Menuet

EARLY SPRING

Sing the magnolia
embrace the forsythia
hug the lilac
drink the greens
wrap yourself in the greens of May!

Drown in the pure waters of my pond
yodel with the tree frogs and the new moon
walk to the top of the world to see
the cows and the old horse in the pasture.

Find words to praise early spring,
its tender greens, yellows, blues,
tentative purples, its shades, lights, hopes.
Find words to describe
the infinity of early spring.

Ask spring to please slow down,
stay a while longer.
Tell its gentle breeze to caress my cheeks
let me relish the fresh eggs of May
savor the strawberries, nurture the lupines, peonies,
roses, delphiniums of June.
Dig the stubborn weeds of early spring
paint my soul with the joy of early spring.

I have to find words to describe early spring.

MY GARDEN

. . . is a forest, a jungle, an ecstasy.
My garden is everything I never dared to be.
My garden screams blue, orange, purple and violet
into the sky.
It does everything I never dared to do.

My garden is a scandal of color, a messy orgy.
My garden says to me:
"Come, enjoy me, walk in me, drown in me."
It says everything I never dared to say.

My garden splashes and shouts and clashes.
It is vibrant, disobedient, exuberant.

My garden says to me:
"You thought you were God
and created me in seven years.
Nurture me, love me
or I will swallow you.
You will become a worm in my rich soil."

Have you ever seen

Have you ever seen anything as beautiful
as my view this early March evening?

The purple blanket that lies over the dark
mountains of New Hampshire far, far away?
The lingering rays of sunshine
crowning the dark tops of white-dotted evergreens?

The low clouds,
clad in threatening grays and gentle pinks,
slumbering in a pale blue sky?

And on the ground the snow so white, so white,
spread out between a black forest on the right,
and on the left skeletal maples, willows and cherry trees,
gentle sentinels?

Trees and clouds, sun and mountains,
light and darkness,

forgive me
for my palette is short of words . . .

THE GOLDFINCH

He knocked on a window one afternoon, yellow,
round, golden and resplendent.
He wanted to come in but I said:
Goldfinch, your wings do not belong in a house,
they belong in the sky; go, fly with the angels.

The next morning at dawn
he knocked on my bedroom window, so I asked:
Goldfinch, are you the soul of the beloved dead,
the spirit of those who will never come back?
I cannot let you in.

Go, fly with the golden multitudes.

IF

If I were a chickadee I would sing louder.
If I were a truck I would drive softer.
If I were Schubert or Mozart I would live longer.
If I were Schubert I would cherish Mozart.

If I were a road I would lead farther.
If I were a dog I would bark lower.
If I were a rooster I would sing Beethoven
                and I would cancel dawn.

If I were a salesman I would call later
                and I would sell dreams.

I would bud earlier if I were a tree,
I would not look back if I were Orpheus.

If God invited me to his table I would ask:
"Are Satan and Judas coming too
                and what's on the menu?"

I would wear a bib and chew on tomorrows.

COURAGE

It was not the fear of heights that kept me silent
and made me hope
ice and snow would pour down from a furious sky.

It was the fear of speaking.

It was not the fear of drowning that kept me silent
and made me hope
the sea would recede and never come back:

It was the fear of speaking.

It was not the fear of death that kept me silent.
It was not the fear of rape that kept me silent.

It was the fear of speaking that kept me silent
when Courage ordered me to speak.

A Walk

I walked on your ashes
at the top of the meadow
where the earth meets the sky.

I looked at the clouds,
at the shadows of the clouds
and the hills far away.

Clouds and shadows,
trees and meadows,
ashes and sky.
You and I.

To Lucy

I love you more than the ocean's surf,
more than the sunset on Mont Blanc.

More than the green, purple, orange,
red hills of New England.

Tucked in bed, beautiful child
with hair almost as white as snow,
eyes sparkling like dark diamonds

that saw monsters under the bed
and far away unclimable peaks.

Miraculous daughter who survived
unimaginable rages
in the depths of the soul.

SPRING CLEANING

Scrub, scrub,
scrub the kitchen floor, the bathroom floor
and the kitchen counters.
Clean the closets of your soul.

Dust, dust,
dust the lamps and the tables,
the bookshelves and the wood stove.
Dust superfluous thoughts.

Wash, wash,
wash the dishes, the windows, the clothes
and the dog's dish.

Wash resentment and lassitude.
Scrub dust clean wash your soul and heart.

The Leopard and the White Star

What would a leopard do with a white star?
Would he look at it with leopard love
and try to jump to the black sky to kiss her?
Would he say "White star you are beautiful and so tender
I would like to take you between my teeth
and chew on you with great tenderness"?
Or would he just stay still in the dark forest,
look at her and write a poem?
Perhaps he would look so hard his neck would develop
what we call in French *torticoli* which would hurt like hell.
Then a big cloud would envelop the white star.
Happy to be freed from the leopard's concupiscent looks
she would laugh and the leopard would cry.

Everything is for the Best in the Best Possible World —*Candide*

Look! The sun is shining! The birds are mating and singing! L. L. Bean is offering gear for outdoor spring adventures! The forsythia buds are ready to explode and say: "Look! The sun is shining! The birds are singing!"

The snow is melting. Think of the beautiful brownish grass waiting to look at the sun. Pretty soon you can look at your garden and imagine all the weeds you'll have to pull out. Look: the sun is shining. The birds are singing. The chickadees chirp and fight around the bird feeders.

Love, peace and hope are everywhere: the Taliban leaders are drinking tea with American soldiers. Michelle Obama is fighting childhood obesity. Nobody knows exactly how she will make pounds and pounds of fat melt from the bodies of cute little children who don't know and whose parents don't know what's good for them, but there is hope!

Look! The sun is shining! Have faith! Have hope! The birds are singing! Soldiers and Talibans are drinking tea together, fat children are losing weight! Everywhere you look there is beauty, even in the dirty snow on both sides of the road, on the mud everywhere and the birds fighting around the bird feeders. The music is playing.

In the Middle of March

What would we be doing if you were here
this evening in the middle of March
when every day a little more snow and ice
      recede into the earth,
when around six a timid sun lingers into the crepuscule,
when the birds sing impatiently
      "Where is my bird feeder?"

Would we be sipping a drink in the living room
talking or not talking, walking up the road holding hands
with a collie, a greyhound or a husky walking between us?

Or perhaps because it is six o'clock one of us
is cooking supper, spaghetti in tomato sauce
or chicken in a curried sauce or a cheese soufflé
      made very carefully,
            almost religiously,
fluffy, light, delicate and savory,
pale yellow like the timid sun of an evening
            in the middle of March.

SLOW

Slow down, spring, slow down.
There is no rush.
Let the buds open their lips leisurely.
Allow them to savor pearls of warm rain
and little drops of sunshine
before they burst into the sky.
Give the tulip's reds and yellows more time
before they shed their rainbows,
bend their wrinkled cheeks and
sink back into the earth.
Let the birds sing the forsythia's
Alleluias and the lilac's Hosannas!
Let my eyes bathe in your tender greens!
Fill my soul with joyful songs of birds,
help me forget the long journey of winter's grief.

Summer

Moderato Suave

BY THE POND

It was there that you stood smiling
a glass in your hand.
Children ran and laughed around the trees,
birds fluttered and chirped in the birches,
the fragrance of freshly ground grass
filled the air.

It was there that I said to myself,
holding a large bowl of spaghetti:
"No matter what he says later,
no matter what he does later,
I shall love him always."

It was there near the pond,
in a sun-filled room,
that you smiled
for the last time and said:
"I don't want to leave you,
I love you."

THE INN

I would like to go with you
to a little inn in Vermont
at the end of a dead-end road.

There is a river and a bridge.

We shall walk in the dead leaves,
have a drink and eat supper
in the restaurant across the muddy road.

We shall discuss the important
and the inconsequential,
enjoy silences.

We shall undress in the room,
make love or go to sleep.

HAPPINESS

On a sunny summer afternoon you said
I think I would enjoy a ride.

I helped you to the car.
We drove slowly through the woods.

We passed the place near the potato field
where the earth meets the sky.

You smiled like a happy child.

At the end of twenty minutes you said
I think we should go back.

I helped you to your bed and you said
Thank you, it was a beautiful ride.

THE TRAVAILS OF A HOUSE OWNER

I put the Bible between Poe and Karl Marx.
I arranged Mary Renault chronologically
and Asterix next to Tintin.

I placed *The American Tradition in Literature*
close to the *Oxford Anthology of English Literature.*

I displayed *Tobacco Road* between *The Wonderland*
and *A Tale of Two Cities* and *The City of God*
at the left of *The Age of Revolution.*

I became so weary of rearranging books,
so tired after rearranging so many unread books
that I installed Simone de Beauvoir
next to *Repairing Your Bicycle*
and Jean-Paul Sartre to the right of Kipling.

WORDS

Chaotic violent or beautiful

let us drink a toast to words
to music and the music of words

to time passing
to the minute that lasts twenty hours

to the gushing of the sea and
years slipping away

to bells and gongs
and to the clicks of the clock

to those who have crossed the gate
and walked into Infinity
to our favorite gods.

Let us sing our songs
in the light of the day
suffer the ocean's rage
till the silence of the night descends.

Do not Worry

I shall watch the cars go by.
Do not fret, do not worry about me.
I shall watch the cars go by.

Do not worry, do not fret,
let your heart rest at peace.
Wait, wait quietly.
I'll be watching the cars go by.

Let your heart rest at peace.
Do not fret: she will come.
She will take you by the hand.
She will lead you to a better place.
Do not fret, do not worry.

I shall watch the cars go by.

I Am

. . . a drop of rain on a dry leaf,
  a tear dripping on a wrinkled cheek,

a word on a blank page,
  a ray of light in a blind face.

I am a spade of earth in the garden,
  a drop of joy in a lost soul,

the sand in the desert,
  a little stone in the river.

I am a molecule, a mountain of joy and laughter,
  a tiny word factory,
  an unfinished symphony.

I am a weed, a tree, a cloud,
I am the sun saying good night.

THESE HANDS

. . . have held so many hands,
typed so many pages,
pealed so many vegetables.

They have been scratched, stung,
bitten, loved and loathed.

These hands soothed suffering limbs,
they dug the earth and washed dishes,
they drove a car and held children.

They groped in darkness and bathed in the sun,
they held on to stones that slid into the stream,
they grabbed dead branches and breaking twigs.

They flirted with dangerous loves,
found comfort in eternal rocks.

Sometimes they reach for the sky,
Sometimes crawl in the forest like dead leaves
or drown in a river between light and darkness.

Autumn

Andante

DEAR LITTLE PEN

What did you write in school today,
dear little pen of mine?
I wrote of tsunamis and earthquakes and
hurricanes and floods and typhoons and
desert storms.
I wrote of devastation in the land.
I wrote of wars upon wars,
bodies upon bodies.
I wrote of flood, of blood, of bodies
without heads, of bodies without limbs.
I wrote of lies, lies, lies upon lies,
money, mountains of money.
I wrote of fake tears,
I wrote of real fears.
I wrote of cold so cold everything changed
into ice and heat so hot the whole world was aflame.
I wrote of hunger, of sick children lying in dirt.
I wrote of mangy dogs in the desert and cannons
blowing down skyscrapers.
I wrote, I wrote, I could not stop until
your hand was paralyzed and
I could write no more.

MOURNING

It is the way things change
how one forgets why they changed
and how they looked.

The face whose lines have faded
the voice that slides into dimness
the chair silent in its sameness.

The indifference of dust
the whiteness of the moon
the cold morning sun blind

to the unseeing eyes,
the body deprived entering
a more simple world.

It is the way things change
and why one forgets how they looked
the grimaces of death on a face.

The smile erased by timelessness
the headless pillow. The empty cup.

NOVEMBER IS HERE, MY LOVE

Except for a few stubborn pink
and yellow snapdragons
the garden has gone to sleep.
Dead pale yellow and dark green leaves scatter
on the gray road.
A few snowflakes wetted my cheeks as I walked
in a gentle breeze.
Tall trees shared years of wisdom
with patches of blue sky and clouds,
black, gray and white.

November is here, my love, and you are dying.
Next to your white bed a small radio plays
Bach and Beethoven.
In the catheter the urine is very red.
I sit next to you and you talk about death.
You are not afraid of death.
Only the whiteness,
the blackness, the solitude of death.

November is here, my love.

THE HOUSE WAS A LANDSCAPE

The house was a landscape with mountains and mushrooms and flowers with grass and snow and a child and a dog and a cat and fish and fishermen and with logs crackling in the stove and with a pensive man with love and conversation now the mountains the mushrooms the flowers are not as they were the grass not so green the snow not so white the fire not so bright the man the child are gone and the days are darker and the house is colder and the meals have lost their flavor the beautiful sounds are muter the loud sounds sound louder and my God the mountains are grayer

THE SHOE

At eight o'clock in the morning
the doctor came to pronounce you dead.

I said I have to put on my shoe.
The doctor said:
"Go, put on your shoe."

GRATING CARROTS ON THE CELLO

When I get old I shall be queen of a small
queendom,
missing the arms of my king
but regretting nothing.

Grating carrots on the A string.

Chickadees, finches, wind blowing in the willows,
daffodils, delphiniums, lilies and sunflowers
will be my courtesans.

I shall visit the sick and teach children.

In the kitchen of my queendom
I will make quiche and soup,
eat some, give some away.

Grating carrots on the D string.

When I get old in my queendom
I will do jumping jacks and sun salutes and
stretch every muscle, every bone
in my old body,
missing my king but regretting nothing.

Grating carrots on the G string.

When the Gate Opened

We climbed so many mountains together
Crossed so many rivers
Walked so many deserts
Swam so many seas.
Side by side we spent so many nights,
Explored Paris, Rome, Athens,
Delphi, Beirut and Tripoli
and nameless, secret villages.
We read so many books
Shared so many thoughts
Entertained so many friends
Cooked so many meals
Enjoyed so many silences.

I took you by the hand
As we walked your last miles together,

Then the gate opened.

Why Do I Write?

Why do I eat, sleep, read, play the cello, exercise, teach French, knit and garden and love my daughter? The answer to these questions is obvious: if I didn't write, read, play the cello, exercise, teach French, garden, knit and love my daughter I would be dead. I would eat and sleep but my soul, my heart and my brain would be dead. I would be a walking zombie.

I write because I frequently would rather write than talk. When you talk you keep bumping into big rocks on the road. You stumble, you fall, you go back and forth, you don't know where you are, you almost forget who you are. When you write, you can gently push that rock, cajole it, walk around it. You can catch yourself when you start falling. You can cancel the whole trip and start all over again in a different direction. Also, you can insult people if you feel like it, swear in the worst way knowing that nobody can hear you.

I write because I like words.

I like words in any language but especially in English and French. I like playing with them, juggling with them, throwing them in the air then letting them fall and bounce to and fro on the ground like a tennis ball.

What am I saying? Do I really love words and do words love me? Are they really my friends? It depends. I hate them when they disobey me. I love them when they sing and tell the truth. I hate them when they spit obscene and ugly lies.

And that leads me to wonder how people who don't read, play the cello, exercise, teach French, garden, knit and love their daughter can live. Do they just eat, sleep and watch television? Do they live without words? But I am changing the subject. I must put my words in a drawer or in the trash.

A Night in Late Autumn

It is time to die.

Time to forsake the orange, brown,
red and purple, green, golden
and yellow fireworks of October.

Time to think about warm days and
cold days, the tender greens of summer,
the brutal winds of winter, time
to build a fire and wear sweaters.

The time has come to pause in gray,
to rake the leaves,
close the doors, bring in wood,
prepare the shovel and the salt.

It is time to welcome darkness, solitude,
melancholy and the howling of coyotes
in the silence of the night.

Colophon

The typeface used for the text
in this book is the venerable
Goudy Old Style, although
Hiroshige contributed to the
titles and Yani offered up a
few sweet swashes.

www.ingramcontent.com/pod-product-compliance
Lightning Source LLC
LaVergne TN
LVHW010030070426
835508LV00005B/287